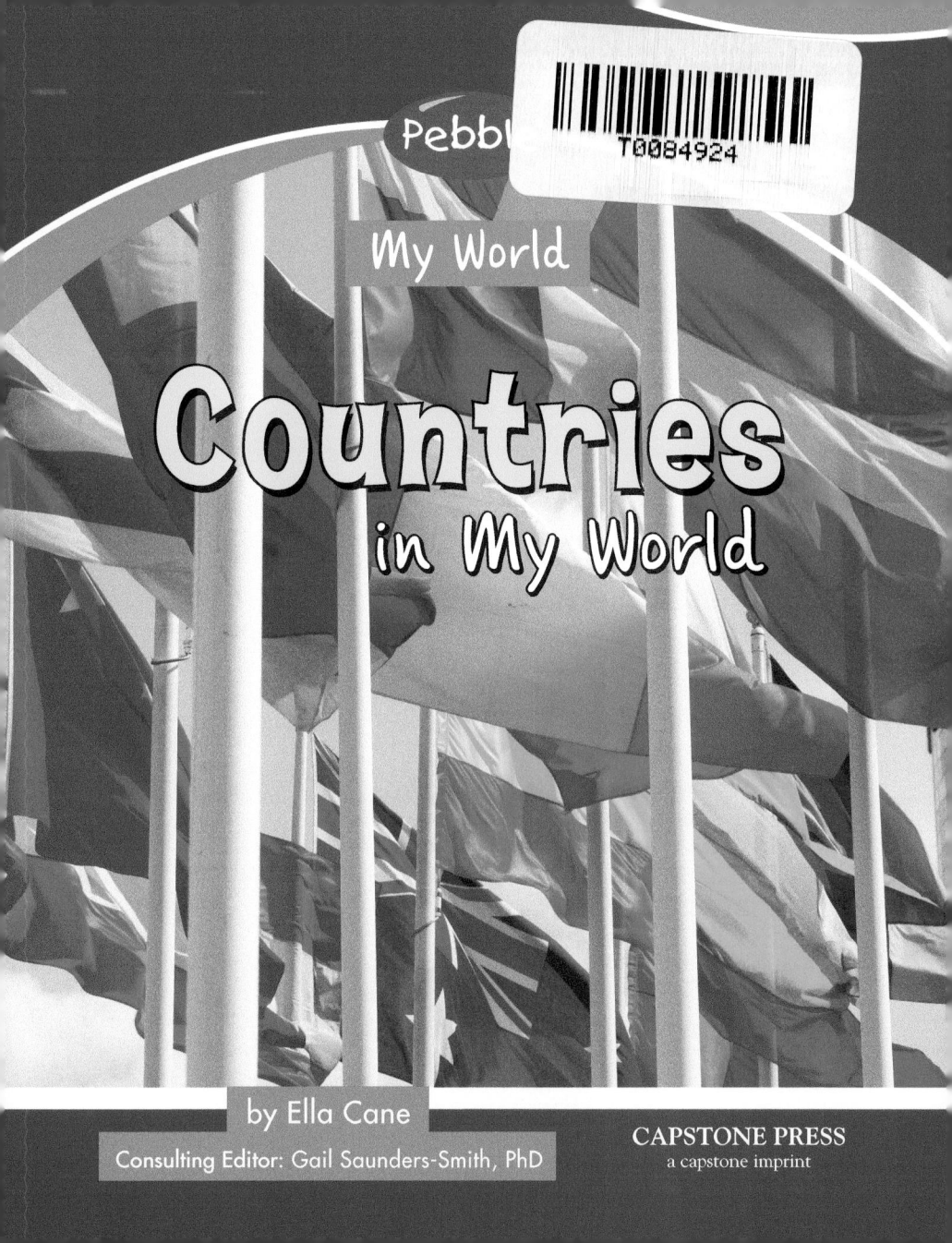

T0084924

Pebbl

My World

Countries in My World

by Ella Cane

Consulting Editor: Gail Saunders-Smith, PhD

CAPSTONE PRESS
a capstone imprint

Pebble Books are published by Capstone Press,
1710 Roe Crest Drive, North Mankato, Minnesota 56003
www.capstonepub.com

Copyright © 2014 by Capstone Press, a Capstone imprint. All rights reserved. No part of this publication may be reproduced in whole or in part, or stored in a retrieval system, or transmitted in any form or by any means, electronic, mechanical, photocopying, recording, or otherwise, without written permission of the publisher.

Library of Congress Cataloging-in-Publication Data
Cane, Ella.
Countries in my world / by Ella Cane.
pages cm. — (Pebble books. My world)
Includes index.
ISBN 978-1-4765-3122-9 (library binding)
ISBN 978-1-4765-3464-0 (paperback)
ISBN 978-1-4765-3470-1 (ebook pdf)
1. Geography—Juvenile literature. I. Title.
G133.C24 2014
910—dc23 2013005990

Summary: Simple text and full-color photographs introduce countries to the reader.

Note to Parents and Teachers

The My World set supports national curriculum standards for social studies related to people, places, and environments. This book describes and illustrates countries. The images support early readers in understanding the text. The repetition of words and phrases helps early readers learn new words. This book also introduces early readers to subject-specific vocabulary words, which are defined in the Glossary section. Early readers may need assistance to read some words and to use the Table of Contents, Glossary, Read More, Internet Sites, and Index sections of the book.

Printed in the United States 5469

Table of Contents

What Is a Country? 5
Government 7
Language 9
Money 11
People 13
Size 15
Landforms 17
Number of Countries 21

Glossary 22
Read More 23
Internet Sites 23
Index 24

United States

What Is a Country?

A country is a piece
of land with borders.
But it's more than that.
Let's take a look at
some countries.

SEAL OF THE PRESIDENT OF THE UNITED STATES

Government

Each country has
a government.
In the United States,
people elect a president
as leader.

ARRÊT
STOP

Language

Many countries have an official language. Canada has two. They are French and English.

Money

Most countries have an official currency. In the United States, it's the U.S. Dollar.

Shanghai, China

People

The world has more than 7 billion people. China is the country with the most people. There are 1.3 billion people in China.

Siberia, Russia

Size

China may have people,
but Russia has space.
Russia is the country
with the most land area.

Landforms

The land in any country is marked with landforms. Mount Everest is part of the countries of China and Nepal.

Some landforms cover several countries. The Sahara desert stretches across countries in northern Africa.

Number of Countries

The world has about 195 countries. This number changes as countries change. What do you know about your country?

Glossary

area—the total surface within a set of borders

border—the dividing line between two places

currency—the type of money a country uses

elect—to choose someone as a leader by voting

government—the group of people who make laws, rules, and decisions for a city, country or state

landform—a natural feature of the land

language—the way people speak or talk

official—having the approval of a country or certain group

Read More

Hirsch, Rebecca. *North America.* Rookie Read-About Geography. New York: Children's Press, 2012.

Hutmacher, Kimberly M. *Mountains.* Natural Wonders. Mankato, Minn.: Capstone Press, 2011.

Roop, Peter, and Connie. *China.* A Visit to. Chicago: Heinemann Library, 2008.

Internet Sites

FactHound offers a safe, fun way to find Internet sites related to this book. All of the sites on FactHound have been researched by our staff.

Here's all you do:

Visit *www.facthound.com*

Type in this code: 9781476531229

Check out projects, games and lots more at
www.capstonekids.com

Index

Africa, 19
China, 13, 17
currency, 11
governments, 7
landforms, 17, 19
languages, 9
largest country in area, 15
most populated country, 13
Mount Everest, 17
Nepal, 17
number of countries, 21
population, 13
presidents, 7
Russia, 15
Sahara, 19
United States, 7, 11
U.S. Dollar, 11

Word Count: 154
Grade: 1
Early-Intervention Level: 17

Editorial Credits
Shelly Lyons, editor; Juliette Peters, designer; Marcie Spence, media researcher; Eric Manske, production specialist

Photo Credits
Capstone Studios: Karon Dubke, 10; Shutterstock: _EG_, 14, Alexander Raths, 20 (bottom), Arsgera, 16, Christopher Halloran, 6, Eniko Balogh, 18, FER737NG, 8, Intrepix, cover, Kotomiti Okuma, 1, TonyV3112, 12, Vitoriano Junior, 4, 20 (top)